BEETROOT

Christopher Trotter

Photography by Caroline Trotter

© Christopher Trotter 2013

Published by Momentum publishing

A CIP catalogue record for this book is available from the British Library.

ISBN 978-0-9926830-0-9

Produced by Print & Design, University of St Andrews
Website: www.st-andrews.ac.uk/printanddesign

Printed by Charlesworth Press, Flanshaw Way, Wakefield, WF2 9LP
Website: www.charlesworth.com

Distributed by Christopher Trotter
Tel: 07739049639

CONTENTS

INTRODUCTION

In this first book of our series of little vegetable books I have chosen beetroot as it is one of my favourite vegetables and for it's remarkable versatility. In her wonderful book *Food in England,* Dorothy Hartley exhorts us not to peel or scrape beetroot as it bleeds easily, and yes she is right, but this should not stop us boiling, baking, roasting, grating, and chopping this marvellous food. The juice does run freely, but just make sure that you add beetroot last to mixed dishes so as not to dye everything and don't wear a white T shirt when preparing. When young and small beetroot needs no peeling or cooking and when old and aged it makes great soups or roasts. A vegetable for all seasons.

My early memories of it are as a horrible condiment, pickled in vinegar and so sharp and unpleasant at to loose any flavour or sweetness of its own. So my love of the beet has come relatively late. I also think that the ready cooked beetroots in vac pac bags are very overcooked so please try to cook your own, as it is very easy. You can also use the stalks and leaves so nothing is wasted.

In this collection of recipes I have tried to show the range of this underestimated vegetable, combining it with ingredients such as hare and venison through to apples, spices, cheese and smoked fish. My good friend Katie Dick has provided some words on its amazing nutritional qualities, and of course my wife Caroline and I have had a lovely time taking the pictures trying to avoid pink fingers on lenses! So here then is a start for everyone you know who says "Oh I never know what to do with beetroot". Well here is the answer.

THE NUTRITIONAL VALUE OF BEETROOT

by Katie Dick

Nutritional Therapist, Healthy reaction
Katie@healthyreaction.co.uk

As a child of the 1960's I remember the fabulous red/purple/violet/blue colours in my beetroot stained tie-dye t-shirt so I am well aware of the warning from Christopher about not using a white top while preparing his recipes! As a nutritional therapist I now know that this deep pigment is partly responsible for the nutritional qualities of this fabulous vegetable.

Romans cultivated beets for their leaves and introduced the plant to northern Europe. These leaves, like others from the *Chenopodiaceae* family such as spinach and chard, are rich in beta carotene antioxidants and are a great source of calcium, iron, and vitamin C. Several of Christopher's recipes such a the risotto and salads can help you enjoy the benefits of these slightly bitter and beautiful beet tops today.

Over time, the root became valued for its sugar content and subsequent claims were made for its ability to 'aid digestion', 'cleanse the liver' and to 'enhance stamina'. Now in the era of scientific rigour these claims are being put to the test by quality investigations and whilst to date there is still some way to go before health claims can be made for this food, early results from research show promise in identifying the mechanisms which may account for beetroot's reputation.

The root is rich in fibre, folic acid, potassium and low in fat, but what interests researchers at the university of Exeter is it's particularly high nitrate content and the anecdotal reports of elite athletes who use beetroot juices to enhance their performance. In 2013 researchers there identified the nitrate as the active ingredient underpinning the observed physiological and exercise benefits.

Several researchers are investigating the betanins found in beetroot. These phytochemicals are responsible for the colour of the common purple variety and the less common golden yellow or white varieties, and early research suggests they may also increase the activity of particular liver enzymes involved in the remove of toxins. If proven, this may account for its reputation as a 'liver cleanser'.

Betains have also shown promise in early studies as an anti-inflammatory mediator, an antioxidant and, through a number of different mechanisms including increasing the activity of some specific immune cells called Natural Killer Cells, it may also be cancer protective.

At Barts and the London School of Medicine researchers are also investigating beetroot, this time focusing on cardiovascular health and blood pressure. Very promising results suggest that concentrated beetroot juice may be able to lower blood pressure in just a few hours.

Clearly all this research is in its early days and the occasional study does not evidence make, so be clear that this is not a signal for those with hypertension to switch to beetroot to control their blood pressure! However, but there is certainly enough evidence here and in the pipeline to suggest that including beetroot in your diet may well bring a wide range of nutrients which work in a variety of ways to promote good health and given time and funding and the political will, one day we may know more.

SEASONS

Guy Watson at Riverford farm in Devon, several of whose recipes I have borrowed and adapted for this book, has been an inspiration to me for many years. His down to earth no nonsense approach to growing organically has been rewarded recently with the Farmer of the year award. In his book *The Riverford farm Cook book* he talks about a first sowing of beetroot in February under glass, then planted out in April for picking in July with subsequent sowings allowing him to crop until November when they are stored over winter keeping well until April. So that's a good indication of availability of British beetroot. Of course you can always buy imported beetroot but if you want to try to buy and cook seasonally then his is the plan to follow.

BUYING AND STORING

For best results, buy in season and buy fresh, please don't be tempted by the vac pac stuff, as its invariably overcooked and disappointing and I have already expressed my dislike of the pickled variety, but each to their own!

Look for smaller ones especially if in season, and often they will come with the leaves still attached, a good sign of freshness, often tied in bunches with string.

Mature ones will keep for several weeks in a cool place so long as they have not been damaged. The tops need to be used right away, remember they can be used just like chard or spinach. If you don't plan to use them then twist them off so they don't draw out the water from the beets but don't cut them.

COOKING

I am giving two main ways of cooking beetroot, which then can be used in other dishes which are signified "Roast" or "Boiled" as part of the ingredients in each recipe. But as with all recipes in this booklet they are to be developed. For me cooking is all about knowing the basics and some techniques and then experimenting from there!

Summer Harvest
Cold Pressed Rapeseed Oil

Healthy, versatile & 100% natural
Low in saturated fat
A source of omega 3

Ideal for dressings, stir-fries &

Produce of Scotland

ROAST BEETROOT WITH THYME

This is a standard fail safe method of cooking beetroot, some people add a little water and no oil, but I am content with the following.

INGREDIENTS

1kg beetroots washed and trimmed
2 sprigs of fresh thyme
4 tblsp Summer Harvest rapeseed oil
2 tsp coarse sea salt

METHOD

1   Pre heat the oven to 200C gas mark 6 and place the beetroots into a roasting tin.
2   Pour on the oil and sprinkle in the salt rolling the beets around to coat them.
3   Throw on the thyme and cover with foil and roast until just cooked, a sharp knife should pierce the flesh but meet a little resistance. Small ones will take about 45 minutes, large, an hour.
4   Allow to cool and rub the skins off with your fingers, use a small knife to remove the root and top.

BOILED BEETROOT

For dishes where no trace of oil is wanted nor indeed the extra flavour of thyme, but what's not to like about thyme? For those who have an Aga or other range cooker bring to the boil on the hob top then transfer to a lower oven.

INGREDIENTS

1 kg beetroots washed and trimmed
1 tsp salt
Water

METHOD

1   Place in a pan cover with water and add salt.
2   Bring to the boil and reduce to a simmer.
3   Small ones will take about 20 minutes and larger 45.
4   Leave to cool in the water and then simply slip them out of their skins in the water.
5   Do not remove them from the water until completely cold otherwise they can dry out.

BEETROOT WITH WHITE SAUCE

One of my earliest memories of eating beetroot, with the contrasting colours creating a gorgeous pink where the beetroot juice seeped in to the sauce, simplicity itself and a delicious stand by. It is also very good with baby beets, ideal to make with freshly cooked beetroots as they can be simply slipped out of their skins, sliced and placed in a dish and have the sauce poured over.

INGREDIENTS

1 shallot or half a small onion studded with two cloves
Bay leaf
Small sprig thyme
400ml milk
300g boiled beetroot
25g butter
25g plain white flour
½ tsp mustard
Salt and pepper

METHOD

1   Heat the milk in a pan to just under boiling with the shallot, bay and thyme. Set aside to infuse for at least 10 minutes.
2   Slice the beetroots and layer in a serving dish.
3   In a saucepan melt the butter over a low heat, and add the flour stir for a couple of minutes.
4   Strain the milk through a sieve into the butter and flour mixture (called a roux) and stir to thicken and form a smooth sauce. Season and add the mustard. Pour over the beetroots and serve.
5   If using cold beetroot then once you have poured over the sauce, place in a hot oven for about 15 minutes to heat through.

BEETROOT AND APPLE SOUP

I have been making beetroot soup for years and have always loved the rich deep colour and earthy flavour, but recently I had a rather sad couple of apples lurking in my kitchen so I just added them and the result was extraordinary some how just accentuating the sweetness of the beetroot. So I always add apples now!

INGREDIENTS

2 tblsp Summer Harvest rapeseed oil
1 large onion 300g approx peeled and sliced
350 g raw beetroot peeled and roughly chopped
1 potato 150 g approx, peeled and chopped
2 dessert apples peeled, cored and chopped
1.3 litres chicken or vegetable stock
1 tsp sea salt

METHOD

1   Soften the onions gently in a pan with the oil.
2   Stir in the beetroot and potatoes, coating with the oil, cover and cook gently for 5 minutes or so.
3   Add the apples and stir to heat through.
4   Pour on the stock, season with salt and bring to the boil, simmer for half an hour or until soft.
5   Allow to cool slightly and liquidise.
6   Serve with some sour cream or crème fraiche with grated raw beetroot.

BORTCHOK

This is a delightful recipe from the former owner of a hotel we ran on Loch Awe, a deer stalking region and the simple combination of game stock and beetroot is an easy way of creating a rich consommé. Don't worry of you don't have game stock a chicken one will suffice but do try to make your own.

INGREDIENTS

500 ml clear game stock
3 raw beetroots @ 300 g grated (skin and all)
Salt and pepper
4 tsp crème fraiche or yoghourt
1 tblsp chopped chives

METHOD

1   Put the stock into a pan and add the beetroots.
2   Bring to a boil, add salt and pepper and simmer for an hour.
3   Strain through a sieve, but don't press the pulp just leave it to drip for a few minutes.
4   Return the soup to the heat and check for seasoning.
5   Serve in hot bowls with a blob of crème fraiche and some chopped chives.

ROASTED RED AND GOLD BEETROOT

Gold beetroot is not easy to find and is perhaps best grown in your own garden. We are lucky in Fife to have Bruce Bennett's Pillars of Hercules in Falkland where he does grow it organically. The two combined in this simple salad look very attractive.

INGREDIENTS

500g golden beetroot
500g red beetroot
80g sunflower seeds
90ml maple syrup (3 tblsp)
1 tblsp wine or sherry vinegar
4tblsp extra virgin olive oil
2 crushed garlic cloves
Fresh herb leaves as garnish
60g baby chard, rocket or young beetroot leaves
Salt and black pepper

METHOD

1   Roast the beetroots in an oven as per the master recipe.
2   Toast the sunflower seeds in a dry pan until lightly coloured.
3   Blend the syrup, vinegar, oil and garlic to form a dressing.
4   Peel the beetroots, or rub off skin with your hands, and cut into even size pieces, mix with the chosen green leaves and dress with the sunflower seeds and dressing and season to taste, garnish with the herbs.

BEETROOT ROESTI

A simple take on the classic Swiss idea. I use a pan with a 26cm diameter I experimented with a cooked beetroot version for radio Scotland's Kitchen Garden programme but presenter Pennie Latin and producer Gillian Russell thought the raw might be better! So ladies, here you are.

INGREDIENTS

200g beetroot peeled, grated and squeezed out.
500g potatoes peeled, grated and squeezed out
Salt and pepper
2 tblsp Summer Harvest rapeseed oil

METHOD

1   Heat a tblsp of oil in the pan.
2   Dry the potato further in a tea towel and then season with salt and pepper.
3   Place half the grated potato in the pan and press down gently especially at the edges.
4   Place the beetroot on top again pressing down to make an even cover over the potato. Season lightly.
5   Place the remaining potato on top and press down again and neaten the edges so no bits stick out. Sprinkle a little more oil over.
6   Lower the heat and allow to cook for 5 minutes. Shake the pan gently and the roesti will loosen.
7   Place a baking tray on top and with care turn the whole thing over! It should be a lovely golden brown.
8   Slide the roesti back in to the pan brown side up and finish cooking, another 10 minutes.

Soufflés are straightforward if you consider the science and make sure the variables are all as they should be:

HEAT – oven temperature is crucial so make sure the oven is up to temperature before you put a soufflé in, the basic mixture also needs to be at room temperature.

CLEAN – the bowl for whisking the egg whites must be clean or else the whites wont fill with as much air as they can so use a glass or stainless steel bowl to beat them, a plastic one may still retain an oily ness from previous preparations. This will make either one large soufflé or 6 individual ones in ramekins, in which case reduce cooking time to 20 minutes.

BEETROOT SOUFFLE

Once again the stunning colour of beetroot really makes this a wonderful dish and it's so simple to make.

INGREDIENTS

40g butter
40g plain flour (plus extra for preparing the soufflé dish)
300ml full fat milk
Bay leaf, sprig thyme
1/8th tsp allspice
Salt and pepper

1 tsp mustard
160g grated raw beetroot (squeezed to remove excess moisture)
2 tsp grated hard cheddar
4 eggs
1 egg white

METHOD

1   Heat the milk in a pan with the herbs until just about boiling and then remove from heat, keep warm.

2   Separate the eggs putting the whites plus the extra white in a large clean glass or stainless steel bowl.

3   Melt the butter in a pan over a low heat and stir in the flour, and cook gently for a few minutes without colouring. Strain the warm milk onto the butter/flour mixture and stir until it thickens. Add the seasonings, mustard, beetroot, and egg yolks, beating in thoroughly.

4   Prepare a 1.2 litre soufflé dish by buttering thoroughly inside with a little softened butter using a pastry brush, finish by brushing upwards from base to top, this helps the soufflé to rise evenly upward. Dust lightly with plain flour.

5   Turn the oven to 200C gas mark 6.

6   Beat the eggs whites with a pinch of salt, which helps to strengthen the albumen, until they form peaks, then fold a third into the beetroot mixture, then carefully pour the beetroot mixture back into the egg white bowl, and gently fold in to combine. Pour in to the prepared soufflé dish sprinkle on the cheese and place in the hot oven; reduce the temperature to 180C gas 4. Cook for up to 40 minutes but DON'T open the door for at least the first 15 or else the soufflé will fall! The soufflé should be brown and crisp on top, well risen and slightly gooey in the middle.

SADDLE OF HARE WITH BEETROOT

This is one of only two specifically meat based dishes and is worth including, even if hares are quite rare, because if you ever get one, then this is the way to cook the saddle! The colour is a cardinal red, and is a truly magnificent combination of flavours. **NB** You need to start this recipe the day before you require it.

INGREDIENTS

2 Saddles of hare
2tsp Olive oil
350g boiled beetroots sliced thinly
2 tablespoons chopped shallot
2 tablespoons wine vinegar
200ml double cream
1 tsp mustard
2 tsp chopped chives

Marinade:
500ml red wine
1 carrot and onion
(cut into small dice)
Sprig rosemary, thyme and
a bay leaf
Salt
8 peppercorns
8 juniper berries
2 cloves garlic crushed

METHOD

1   With a flexible knife, remove the membrane covering the saddles.
2   Marinade them with the wine, vegetables, herbs, peppercorns juniper berries and garlic for about a day.
3   Take the saddles out of the marinade and dry carefully. Strain the marinade through a sieve, retain.
4   Turn the oven to 250C gas mark 9.
5   Heat the olive oil in an ovenable pan.
6   Dry the saddles on kitchen paper and brown them all over in the hot pan.
7   Put them into the oven for 10 minutes. They should be cooked until still pink. Leave in warm place to rest.
8   Remove most of the fat from the pan and cook the beetroot in it adding the shallot, cook for two minutes to soften.
9   Add the vinegar and 4 tablespoons of marinade, reduce by simmering for a minute, add the cream, mustard and seasoning and reduce until a coating consistency is achieved. Keep warm.
10 To serve, remove the fillets from top and bottom, and slice lengthways, dress on 4 plates and arrange the beetroot on top reheat the sauce but do not boil, and spoon it over.

FILLET OF VENISON WITH BEETROOT AND GHERKINS

This is a simple but rich dish taken from my book The Scottish Kitchen that I wrote for the National Trust for Scotland. If you cannot get fillet then a piece from the loin will do equally well.

INGREDIENTS

450g fillet of venison (red deer)
Salt and black pepper
1 tbsp Summer Harvest rapeseed oil
50g butter
1 shallot peeled and finely chopped
175 g boiled, peeled beetroot
1 tblsp chopped beetroot stalks
50g gherkins
3 tbsp red wine
115 ml dark stock

METHOD

1   Dry the fillet thoroughly and season with salt and pepper. Heat a pan and add the oil and half the butter; when very hot place the fillet in the pan and brown all over. Reduce the heat, cover and cook gently for 10 minutes.
2   Meanwhile, cut the beetroot into slices then slice them into matchstick strips. Do the same with the gherkins.
3   Remove the meat from the pan and keep it warm. Pour away the excess fat from the pan, add the chopped shallot and beetroot stalks, stirring into the juices. Add the beetroot matchsticks, and increase the heat and pour in the wine and stock, reduce by half.
4   Away from the heat swirl in the remaining cold butter, set aside.
5   Slice the fillet at an angle divide between serving plates pour over sauce. I have put mine here on some wilted ruby chard – very yum!

BEETROOT AND POTATO CAKES

This is a sort of bubble and squeak only using beetroot instead of cabbage. It can of course be simply cooked together and served as a hash but this some how adds to its dignity. I find this a useful way of using up ends of beetroot or even cooked pieces.

INGREDIENTS

2 tblsp Summer Harvest rapeseed oil
1 medium onion peeled and sliced
200g raw beetroot, peeled and shredded
200g mashed potato
1 tsp horseradish sauce
Seasoned flour
Tsp butter

METHOD

1   Over a medium heat fry the onion in a frying pan with the rapeseed oil and then add the beetroot, cover and cook for about 5 minutes to soften, stirring from time to time.
2   Add the balsamic vinegar, cover again and cook gently for another 5 minutes.
3   Add to the mashed potato, and add the horseradish.
4   Form into 6 cakes and chill.
5   Roll in the seasoned flour and fry gently in a pan with the rapeseed oil and butter. Brown on one side – about 5 minutes, turn over and cook 'til hot through.

BEETROOT WEDGES

Ideal for young fresh beets, as they don't need to be peeled and provide finger food for summer eating with dips or just a side dish for a barbeque.

INGREDIENTS

8 beetroots approx 80 – 100 g each
2 tblsp Summer Harvest rapeseed oil
Sprig fresh thyme, leaves pulled off
Sprig fresh rosemary, leaves pulled off
2 tsp coarse salt

METHOD

1   Set oven to 200C gas mark 6.
2   Wash and top and tail beetroots.
3   Cut into 6 wedges.
4   Place in a bowl with the herbs and their stems.
5   Mix with the salt.
6   Place in a roasting tray and roast for 15 – 20 minutes tuning occasionally until browning at the edges.

BEETROOT TATIN

Apples have traditionally been the ingredient in a Tatin from when the famous "Tante" dropped her apple tart, but I have used shallots successfully as a first course, so here is a version with beetroot, I think the vinegar helps to bring out the sweetness. But if you are a Tatin hand then by all means use the traditional butter and sugar version and serve as a pudding! Go on be a rebel.

INGREDIENTS

4 oz short crust pastry
5- 6 small raw beetroots
15g butter
1 tblsp summer harvest rapeseed oil
1 tblsp wine vinegar
3 tsp soft brown sugar

METHOD

1   Wash the beetroots and top and tail them and make sure they are dry.
2   Heat the pan and add the butter, oil, vinegar and sugar, bring to a simmer.
3   Cut the beetroots in half through the circumference and place cut side down in to the pan make sure you pack them tightly so there are no gaps but they must all be touching the pan base.
4   Cook gently for about 10 minutes.
5   Roll out the pastry to a disc that will fit the pan and carefully place over the top of the pan, tucking it into the pan to cover the beetroots snugly.
6   Bake in the oven for 15 minutes or until pastry is set and lightly browned.
7   Allow to cool slightly then turn out onto a waiting hot plate and serve with a salad.

BEETROOT BAKED WITH CREAM AND ROSEMARY

Another idea adapted from the wonderful Riverford team. Excellent on its own as a first course or to accompany a roast. If you have fresh garlic then simply peel and slice it and mix with the sliced beetroots before arranging in the gratin dish.

INGREDIENTS

1 kg boiled peeled beetroot
3 cloves garlic peeled and crushed with a little salt
200 mls double cream
2 sprigs fresh rosemary
Salt and pepper

METHOD

1   Turn the oven to 180C gas mark 4.
2   Place the rosemary in a small pan with the cream and bring to a boil and remove from the heat, leave to infuse.
3   Slice the beetroots thinly and mix in a bowl with the garlic, salt and pepper.
4   Arrange in a gratin dish and strain the cream over the top.
5   Place in a hot oven for 20 minutes until bubbling.

SPICED BEETROOT WITH CUMIN AND COCONUT MILK

One of my favourite spices is cumin as it seems to enhance sweetness in things and is not so overpowering as to mask flavours. I experimented initially with potatoes and spices but realised that beetroot would also benefit especially older beets or over wintered ones.

INGREDIENTS

1 tblsp Summer Harvest rapeseed oil
1 tsp brown mustard seeds
1 onion peeled and sliced
2 red chillies (seeds removed and finely sliced)
2 cloves garlic crushed with salt
2 tsp ground cumin
½ tsp turmeric
¼ tsp cinnamon

500 g raw beetroot (peeled and cut into cubes)
4 ripe tomatoes (blanched and skinned then chopped)
100 ml coconut milk
Juice of a lime
Handful of roughly chopped flat parsley

METHOD

1   Take a large pan and cook the mustard seeds gently in the oil 'til they pop.
2   Add the onion and chillies and stir to soften.
3   Add the garlic and spices and stir together for a few minutes making sure the garlic doesn't burn.
4   Stir in the beetroot and cook for another few minutes.
5   Add the tomatoes and enough water to cover the base of the pan by a centimetre. Simmer gently for 20 minutes until the beetroot is just cooked.
6   Pour in the coconut milk and simmer 'til it thickens slightly, add lime juice and salt and pepper.
7   Serve with the parsley strewn over the top.

BEETROOT RISOTTO

Risotti are the most wonderful of dishes, as once you have the basic technique mastered you can add whatever you like. Apart from the amazing colour in this dish the simplicity of just the beetroot and cheese works well. Try adding smoked bacon with the leek or perhaps some chopped beetroot stalks, and the leaves torn up and folded in at the end just before the cheese.

INGREDIENTS

1.5 litres chicken or vegetable stock
2 tblsp unsalted butter
2 leeks cut into a dice
2 medium raw beetroots
400g Arborio rice
125ml dry white wine
Salt and ground black pepper
1 tblsp Summer Harvest rapeseed oil
50g Anster cheese

METHOD

1   Heat the stock to boiling point and keep on a gentle simmer. In a heavy based pan melt the butter over a medium heat and add the leek and cook gently until softened.
2   Peel and grate the beetroot and stir in.
3   Add the rice and stir well to coat with all the ingredients.
4   Add the wine and stir until it has been absorbed.
5   Now begin to add the stock, a ladle full at a time, stirring constantly and making sure that the liquid is all absorbed before adding the next ladle.
6   The rice should be tender but still firm to bite, add water if you run out of stock before this moment is reached. Take off the heat and stir in the rapeseed oil and cheese.

BEETROOT WITH SESAME SEEDS AND BALSAMIC VINEGAR

I love just eating these in my fingers, the sticky tangy dressing foiled by the rich almost smoky flavour of the sesame seeds. It's great with roasts or with dips or cold as a side with curry. I have even used a few remaining pieces in a soup where it added a smoky depth.

INGREDIENTS

500g small raw beetroot
2 tblsp honey
2 tblsp balsamic vinegar
2 tblsp sesame seeds

METHOD

1   Turn the oven to gas 6 180C.
2   Trim the beetroots and cut into quarters or sixths tip into a roasting tray and pour over the honey and balsamic.
3   Roast for about 20 minutes, shaking the tray to keep the beets coated until cooked and the dressing sticky.
4   Meanwhile toast the sesame seeds in a dry pan over a medium heat, turning occasionally to create an even colouring.
5   When ready place the beetroots in a bowl and sprinkle over the seeds.

SALAD WITH BEETROOT ORANGE, BACON AND CARAWAY — SERVED WARM

Introducing yet more beetroot friendly ingredients, and if inclined you can avoid the bacon or even use smoked beetroot instead! James at East Pier Smokehouse St Monans does this (I think it's a little over cooked!).

INGREDIENTS

300g boiled peeled beetroot
1 tblsp Summer Harvest rapeseed oil
4 rashers of streaky bacon
2 tsp caraway seeds
Clove of garlic crushed to a pulp
Juice and zest of an orange
1 tsp brown sugar
3 oranges peeled and sliced
Salt and black pepper

METHOD

1   Slice the beetroots into about four then cut the slices into chunky batons.
2   Cut the bacon into thin lardons.
3   Heat a pan and add the oil, when hot fry the bacon until lightly browned and set aside.
4   Add the caraway seeds and stir for a few minutes.
5   Reduce the heat and stir in the garlic and add the sugar and orange, just bring to a boil.
6   Add the beetroots, warm through and add the orange slices, remove from heat season and gently mix through.
7   Serve on four plates with the bacon strewn on the top.

SMOKED SALMON WITH BEETROOT AND LIME RELISH

It's the lime and honey combination that provides the backdrop for our hero here. Dill and cucumber provide a sort of Scandinavian influence and boy does the smoked salmon work! But please buy the best, none of your mass produced pulpy stuff. Try Inverawe from Argyll.

INGREDIENTS

1/2 tblsp runny honey
1 tblsp finely chopped dill
1 lime grated and juiced
255g boiled beetroot
1/2 peeled cucumber
Salt and pepper
300g sliced smoked salmon

METHOD

1   Mix together the honey lime juice and zest.
2   Trim and peel the beetroot and cut into fine matchsticks.
3   Slice the cucumber into rounds and then into matchsticks.
4   Slice the smoked salmon into strips.
5   Gently combine all the ingredients with the dressing and season with salt and pepper.

REMOULADE WITH COLD SMOKED TROUT

A delicious variation on traditional celeriac remoulade. I love the colours here as the trout has a brighter colour than salmon and if you mix them carefully the beetroot doesn't completely stain the celeriac and mayonnaise.

INGREDIENTS

Half a celeriac @ 450g
Juice of a lemon
150 g raw beetroot
3 tblsp mayonnaise
1 tsp Dijon mustard
250 g Cold smoked trout (Inverawe's is excellent)

METHOD

1   Peel and grate the celeriac and mix it with the lemon juice to prevent discolouring.
2   Peel and grate the beetroot, keep aside.
3   Mix the mayonnaise and mustard into the celeriac, check for seasoning and then gently fold in the beetroot to make sure it doesn't stain too much.
4   Place a small mound in the middle of four plates and drape thinly sliced smoked salmon around, top with a blob of caviar (optional) and serve with a wedge of lemon and brown bread.

BEETROOT TZATZIKI

Frankly given the choice I would always go for this brightly coloured version of this Greek "dip" rather than the pale cucumber version. I suppose that our imported cucumbers are just watery! This however packs a punch.

INGREDIENTS

400g boiled beetroot
250 ml natural yoghourt
½ onion finely chopped
Clove garlic crushed with salt
Zest of lime
3 tsp chopped dill
Salt and pepper

METHOD

1   Peel and grate the beetroot and carefully mix with the remaining ingredients, (phew that was hard).

BEETROOT AND GOATS CHEESE SALAD WITH ROCKET

This is a simple version of a dish I learnt whilst doing a "stage" in Zafferano, a Michelin starred restaurant in London. It served superb Italian food but for this dish they used a centrifugal machine to get the juice and flavour out of the beetroot! Now not everyone has such a kitchen gadget…

INGREDIENTS

4 small boiled beetroots approx 350 g
2 x goat's crottins
Couple of handfuls rocket 40g approx

Dressing:
1 small raw beetroot
3 tblsp balsamic vinegar
6 tblsp Summer Harvest rapeseed oil
¼ tsp mustard

METHOD

1   Cut the beetroots into wedges.
2   Cut the crottins in to wedges.
3   Blitz the raw beetroot in a liquidiser with the balsamic until well pureed mix in the oil and mustard, pass through a sieve check for seasoning.
4   Arrange beetroot and crottins on 4 plates with the rocket in the middle and then dribble the dressing around the plates.
5   Some grated raw beetroot over the top adds a splash of colour and crunch.

APPLE PEAR AND WALNUT SALAD WITH BEETROOT AND BLUE CHEESE

Apples, beetroot and soft cheese work well together and this summery salad combines them all. The beetroot stems make a pretty splash of colour and add crunch.

INGREDIENTS

Juice of a lemon
2 apples with pretty skins
1 pear
500g boiled skinned beetroots
1 tblsp blue cheese crumbled
2 tblsp walnuts broken into small pieces
2 tblsp finely chopped beetroot stems
2 tblsp Summer Harvest rapeseed oil
Chopped chives or marjoram

METHOD

1   Cut the apples in quarters and cut out the cores then slice thinly and mix into the lemon juice.
2   Peel the pear and cut into quarters and core. Cut into small chunks and add to the lemon juice coating to prevent discolouring.
3   Cut the beetroot into sixths or eights depending on size from top to bottom and arrange on a dish or four plates.
4   Arrange the apples and pears, sprinkle over the walnuts and blue cheese.
5   Mix the oil with the remaining lemon juice to form a simple dressing adjust seasoning and dribble over the salad, sprinkle over the chopped stems and the herbs.

BEETROOT CAKE

This most moist of cakes really brings out the sweetness of beetroot, if once you have grated the beets and it's very wet squeeze a little moisture out but not to worry if there isn't much. The cinnamon is a great spice but do experiment with others such as mixed spice.

INGREDIENTS

125ml vegetable oil
125g light brown sugar
175g chopped walnuts
350g grated raw beetroot
225g plain flour, sieved
1tsp baking powder
1 tsp bicarbonate of soda
2 tsp cinnamon
¼ tsp salt
4 eggs

Topping:
300g Philadelphia cream cheese
150g icing sugar
125 ml double cream
Zest of an orange

METHOD

1   Preheat oven to 180C gas mark 4 and line a deep 20cm cake tin with cling film.
2   In a large bowl combine the oil and sugar to form a smooth mixture.
3   Gradually add the dry ingredients to the bowl and beat in each egg thoroughly.
4   Stir in grated the beetroot and chopped walnuts and spoon the mixture into the prepared tin.
5   Place the cake tin in the centre of the oven for 1 hour 10 minutes, or until a skewer, pushed into the centre of the cake comes out clean. Allow the cake to cool on a wire rack.

Topping
Sieve the sugar into a food processor then add the remaining ingredients and whiz to form a spreadable mixture. Spread over the cake.

CHOCOLATE BEETROOT BROWNIES

My wife insisted that her recipe with raw beetroot was better but I disagreed! So this one stands, but there are many ways of cooking a brownie do let us know yours!

INGREDIENTS

250g dark chocolate, broken in pieces
200g unsalted butter
250g cooked beetroot (boiled)
3 eggs
3 drops vanilla essence
200g caster sugar
50g cocoa powder
50g semolina
1 tsp baking powder
100g desiccated coconut

METHOD

1   Preheat the oven to 180C gas 4.
2   Melt the chocolate with the butter in a large bowl over a pan of hot water.
3   Blitz the peeled cooked beetroot in a food processor.
4   Add the eggs, vanilla and sugar process 'til mixed in.
5   Mix the cocoa, semolina, baking powder with the coconut.
6   Fold the beetroot puree in to the chocolate and then fold in the remaining ingredients.
7   Line a tin 28x 18 cm approx with cling film.
8   Pour in the mixture and bake in oven for 30 to 35 minutes.

CHOCOLATE AND BEETROOT ICE CREAM

As with the brownies beetroot and chocolate go well together and ever since a trip to Honduras where we saw Cardamoms grow I use them where I can and I think it provides a lovely depth to this ice cream.

INGREDIENTS

300g roast beetroot
300 ml whole milk
3 cardamom pods
200 ml double cream
4 egg yolks
100g caster sugar
100g dark chocolate

METHOD

1   Heat 200 ml milk with the cardamom to just below boiling and set aside to infuse.
2   Whisk the yolks in a bowl with the sugar until pale then whisk on the hot milk.
3   Rinse milk pan and return the mixture to it. Cook gently stirring all the time to create a custard but don't over cook or it will go grainy. Set aside.
4   Melt the chocolate in a bowl over a pan of hot water, stir into the custard.
5   Puree the beetroot with the remaining 100 ml of the milk, and add to the chocolate custard, strain through a sieve and cool.
6   Freeze in ice cream machine.

BEETROOT WITH AUBERGINE DIP

I was in The Lebanon a few years ago with my friend Jules Akel not only a nice bloke but an experimental cook as well. And although the favoured dip in that country is hummus we also had this delicious one. Jules is a Graphic designer and lives in Dalwhinnie but his family are from Beirut. This recipe is dedicated to him, in memory of our last day in the family village, having breakfast with his distant cousin, feasting on all their own produce, olives, oil, cheese, tomatoes and fruit, such hospitality.

INGREDIENTS

1 aubergine
2 cloves garlic, peeled
2 beetroots 250g approx Boiled
1 tsp sea salt
½ tsp cumin
Juice of a lemon
100ml extra virgin olive oil

METHOD

1   Bake the aubergine in a hot oven for about half an hour until soft to touch.
2   Allow to cool then cut in half and scrape all the insides out.
3   Puree the beetroot with the garlic and salt in a food processor, 'till smooth.
4   Add the aubergine, cumin and lemon juice and puree together.
5   Finally add the oil and scrape down.
6   Serve as a dip with crudités or crisps.

BEETROOT AND ONION MARMALADE

A lovely simple condiment that keeps in the fridge for a while and is delicious with grilled and cold meats amongst other things. You don't need to make this amount, just half everything, but it does keep!

INGREDIENTS

Ingredients
1 Kg onions peeled and sliced
1 Kg raw beetroots
100g fresh root ginger
200ml Summer Harvest rapeseed oil
Zest of two oranges
300 g soft brown sugar
100 ml balsamic vinegar
200 mls wine vinegar
400 mls water

METHOD

1   Peel and slice the beetroot, then cut into strips.
2   Peel and slice the ginger and cut into strips.
3   Combine all ingredients and place in a large pan and bring to the boil.
4   Reduce heat and simmer for an hour and a half until thick and textured.
5   Jar up and store in a cool place.

BIOGRAPHIES

CAROLINE TROTTER is a freelance photographer and works across a wide variety of subjects. Weddings are her main area of work but she also does portraits, both human and animal – horses, dogs etc. Caroline covers events for associations such as Fife Chamber of Commerce and provides business portraits for websites and marketing purposes. She also runs photography courses from home.

www.carolinetrotter.co.uk

CHRISTOPHER TROTTER is Fife's Food Ambassador, an honorary title bestowed on him for his work promoting food from Fife. He is also a freelance chef, cookery writer and food commentator, appearing on programmes such as BBC radio Scotland's Kitchen café and Kitchen garden. As a consultant he has worked with agencies as diverse as Argyll and the Island's Enterprise and The National Trust for Scotland. Christopher also provides cookery classes and food tours and he is passionate about fresh produce in its season.

www.fifefoodambassador.co.uk

They have two children, four hens (currently), two dogs and a mac cat. And live in rural Fife.

ACKNOWLEDGEMENTS

Where do recipes come from? I have helped myself liberally from the *Riverford Farm Cook Book* for which great thanks. Inspirational chefs also include Rowley Leigh of Le café Anglais in London, one of our best, but least known food writers. Anthony Demetre of Arbutus (amongst others) also in London. Bortchok comes from *Lady Maclean's Cook Book*. Other chefs and cooks include Hugh Fearnley-Whittingstall, Hattie Ellis, Bridgid Allen and Yotam Ottolenghi. And of course David Naylor.

Thanks also to Duncan Stewart at St Andrews University Print and Design for realising my idea and to the team at Waterstone's book shop in St Andrews for encouragement. Bruce Bennet (Scotland's Riverford Farm) for his golden beetroot.

Summer Harvest®
Cold Pressed Rapeseed Oil

At 'Summer Harvest', we pride ourselves on producing our Multi-Award Winning Scottish 'Cold Pressed Rapeseed Oil'.

OUR FAMILY FARM

Our 'Cold Pressed Rapeseed Oil' is from a specially selected single variety of seed, which is grown, pressed and bottled on our family farm in the fertile valley of Strathearn in rural Perthshire. Our family have farmed here for over 100 years and have grown oilseed-rape for around 30 years. We have a real focus on the environment and sustainability and this is reflected in our farming techniques. An example of this is our close work with our beekeepers to help create the best environment for bees on our farm.

Perthshire is renowned for its light, fertile farmland and with its long summer days and mild nights provides the perfect conditions for our oil to mature in the seeds. This in combination with our experienced and sensitive farming helps to give our oil its distinctive soft smooth flavour.

OUR OIL

Our seed is simply cold pressed, filtered then bottled, retaining all the natural goodness from the seed. No heat or chemicals are used leaving us with 100% natural oil with the highest quality of taste, colour and healthy goodness.

'Summer Harvest Cold Pressed Rapeseed Oil' has a light, nutty, buttery taste with tones of garden peas or asparagus. Our oils have gained many awards including two 'Scotland Food & Drink Excellence Awards' and five 'Great Taste Awards'.

USES

Due to its delicious light taste and high flash point (230°C), it can be used for marinades, salsas, dipping and dressings, as well as for stir frying and roasting. Furthermore, it is a great dairy free alternative to butter in baking.

HEALTH BENEFITS

As you may know, 'Cold Pressed Rapeseed Oil' is low in saturated fats (6%), high in Omega 3 and 6 and high in vitamin E, a powerful anti-oxidant. Compared to olive oil, 'Summer Harvest Cold Pressed Rapeseed Oil' has approximately half the saturated fats and 10 times the Omega 3. A good balance of Omega 3 and 6 (essential fatty acids) helps to maintain a healthy body and can help to reduce cholesterol levels, which has a positive effect on coronary heart disease.

NOTES